Poems
For
Any
Mood

Poems for any Mood

By

Margot Bish

Poems for laughter
Poems for thought
Poems for imagination
Poems for happiness
Poems for comfort
Poems to motivate
Whatever your mood, there's a
poem here to suit you.

Contents page

Key to letters
F   funny
N   about nature
T   philosophical
S   sad

The rest, I leave to you to describe

The Cat In The Mirror

The cat in the mirror cat lives in the cupboard,
Well, that's what my cat tells me,
But she's very quick at hiding,
So when you look inside it,
She's never there to see,

My cat has tried to creep up,
And pounce from near the wall,
But that clever cat had sneaked away,
And wasn't there that day at all,

She's always there when we wake up,
And greet the day anew,
She eats her breakfast every day when my cat eats
hers, too,
She even cleans when my cat cleans in just the same
way,
And she does this morning, noon and night every
single day,

The first day they met, they were both angry,
Swishing their tails, full of animosity,
So I suggested my cat try a smile and we would see
what we would see,
And, you know that cat, she smiled right back,

And now they're friends, close as can be

Growing Up

Adults don't explain properly,
And laugh when I don't get it right,
But its not my fault if they omit things,
And make me look not bright,

They showed me a photo of "you",
And I wondered who this "you" could be,
I wondered if she'd ever come visiting,
She looked a lot like me,

One day I went hill walking,
With my friend who's an adult, too,
She pointed out a robin, singing,
I laughed,
Said, "Silly old you,
That's not a robin, silly. That's a BIRD,
It has feathers you see",
Well, I didn't know that birds had names,
Just like Mum and Dad and Me,

They asked me what one and three made,
I said, "Thirteen, of course."
If they wanted an answer of four, well ask me

'bout legs on a horse,

Then there's the children in Thytendercare,
That's a country in Africa, I'm sure,
So Jesus must bless and look after them,
And one day, I'll visit them there,
I guess I don't mind them smiling,
So long as the joke is explained,
But it's hard growing up in this strange big world,

When there's so much I still haven't learned,

Scarecrow

I wish I was a scarecrow, standing in a field,
Watching the clouds go by,
I wish I was a scarecrow standing in a field,
Watching the birds flying high,

There'd be a stream at the bottom of the field,
With ducks quack, quacking as they swim,
With frogs on the lily pads and lizards on the
wall,
And me looking after them all,

There'd be trees with their leaves,
Rustling in the breeze,
And me looking after all of these,

I WISH I was a scarecrow standing in a field,
Watching the clouds go by,
I WISH I was a scarecrow standing in a field,
Watching the birds flying high,

Ghost

There's a ghost in the subway,
I'm scared to go through,
I can hear his voice going "Woo,woo,woo,"
There's a ghost in the subway,
I can't get passed,
I turn around and run away very fast,

No one told me he was nice,
Only known to frighten mice,
There's a ghost in the subway,
Going "Woo,woo,woo,"

The Woods

When I go down to the woods, you know,
I see the colours all aglow,
Reds and orange and brown and green,
No place better in the world to see,

I see the birds flying on the breeze,
I hear the wind blowing in the trees,
Listen to the rippling of the stream,
There's no place better in the world to be,

When I go down to the woods, you know,
I see the colours all aglow,
Reds and orange and brown and green,
No place better in the world to see,

I see a robin, breast so red,
I see the fox going home to his bed,
His ears pricked up,his brush held high
I see the buzzard flying by,

Then there's the woodpecker green and red,
Tapping his beak and nodding his head,
I see the badger black and white,
Scurrying home, his eyes so bright,

I hear the song of a cheeky thrush,
Singing it twice from the top of a bush,
His ribald voice so full of cheer
His notes so pure and clear we hear,

I sometimes go on a Winter's night ,
When all is lit in pale moonlight,
The branches lit up clear and bright,
Glistening in the snow so white,

I see a sea of bluebells there,
Can't do nothing but stand and stare,
There's peace here and serenity
There's a lesson there for you and me,

Above the sky's a dash of blue,
I see the sun glinting down on dew,
There are deer, looking at me,
Standing still but running free,

When I go down to the woods, you know,
I see the colours all aglow,
Reds and orange and brown and green,
There's no place better in the world to be.

Bluebells

There are bluebells in the wood,
There are trees soaring high above,
There are birds flying in the sun,
I love each and every one,
There are bluebells in the wood,

There are celandine and stitchwort too,
Depending on your point of view,
These may be the favourite flowers for you,
But for me, the bluebell is,
The bluebell in the wood,

There's peace here, there's serenity,
It's a place where dreams soar free,
Standing here beneath the boughs of the tree,
There are bluebells in the wood,

Afghanistan

"The soldiers are coming!"
I hear them cry,
As I sit in the kitchen, and I wonder why,
My mother holds her hands up to her face
And looks around our sparse furnished space,

"The soldiers are coming!"
More voices loud
And the thud of feet from a running crowd,
"Under the table," my mother says,
And I crawl beneath, just can see her legs,

There's the rattle of guns and tank engines roar,
From the villagers, I hear voices no more,
The village itself seems to hold its breath
Almost I think I might have gone deaf

Except, my mother's weeping now,
Sobs and gasps, breathing fast then slow,
Words of prayer between each gasp
She's praying for me as each word flows,

There's a whistling noise above our heads,

Shock vibrations rattle the beds
A massive thud, I duck my head,
My ears hurt and the ground turns red,

I shut my eyes from the terrible sight
Wish my mother had left me, run away, taken flight,
For now I'm an orphan, just a farmer's boy
sitting under a table, his home blown away,

And Next Door

"The soldiers are coming"
My mother cried,
And looked around for somewhere to hide,
Her face was pale, her eyes opened wide,
Her lip, it trembled, but tears she denied,

Our house is sparse, just two rooms,
No cellar to hide in as danger looms,
"The soldiers are coming,"
My father shouts,
"Get under the table and don't come out,"
I crawl beneath the tablecloth folds,
I'm shivering as if feeling cold,

Machinery whirs, and clanks afar,
Tanks rumble and I feel deep earth jar,
"Why are they here?" I whisper in fear,
But no answer from mum nor dad I hear,

The noise fades to silence,
Drops like a blanket of snow,
We remain like statues, no place to go,
And then a whistle and an echoing thud,
The roof collapses and I'm sprayed with blood,

I cover my ears, my eyes rain tears,
And I scream and scream and scream with fear,
Me, the table the only survivors,
Why do this to me? I cannot see,
We were only farmers,
And I'm only three

Look After Our World

The world we live in is a beautiful place,
Full of mountains and rivers, large fields, open
space,
And as I listen to the songs of birds in the trees,
I wonder why man seeks to bury all these,
Under acres of tarmac and buildings of brick,
When the damage we cause makes us all sick,

After all, we all know that we need oxygen
That we'll die if the air is just carbon, nitrogen,
With hydrogen joining that most precious gas
To make too much water and flood out your
house,

So why don't we start looking after the land?
To survive man, with nature, must go hand in
hand,
Our planet perceives mankind as some kind of
nit,
A parasite to exterminate, a sort of rash or an
itch,

So, she sends out floods and fires and storm,
They are warnings to mankind that its time to
reform,

She sends out disease to end mankind,
Then the world she'll rebuild with other life
forms,
But how sad, in the process innocent creatures
must die, no more hedgehogs, nor puffins, no
bees nor butterflies

No doubt, planet earth will regenerate once more,
From the fungi and algae, from the planet's hot
core,
But how odd to think of that green blue ball
All silent and empty the animals all gone,
Just because man was greedy, all he wanted was
fun,
He heeded not those warnings,
And did nothing but talk, and deceive,
Left the job up to others, 'til there could be no
reprieve,
And then dashed around when its already too late,
Crying out to the earth, "Oh please, can't you
wait?"

But the earth, it was dying and could wait no
more,
For the leaders who raped and pillaged the earth's

floor,
'Til nothing could grow 'neath the sun's fiery
furnace,
And mankind did perish, crisp burned, starved or
drowned.

To The Sea

Can you see the cloud building?
Like a mushroom, but white.
Its climbing mountains,
Taking sunlight

And now, with no sound at all,
the rain falls,

Lands on grass and sheep and walls,
Like an invading army, drops meet
clump together, hurry forwards, then stall,

The cloud climbs higher, goes from white to
black,
And suddenly the rain beats hard on my back,
Hits the floor like ball bearings,

Smashes earth to mud on the track,

Now it hurries and scurries cross the ground,
Making an island of a small grassy mound,
It tumbles into streamlets, and chuckling out
loud,
It dances down waterfalls with power newly
found,

Water roaring,it runs through a gully,
And pours round a boulder each drop in a hurry,
To leave the uplands of their birth.
And whirl and swirl compelled as if by mirth,
To drop from pool to pool, white water rushing,
And as another stream collides,
The river erodes, pushes banks aside,
So much power as droplets join together,
In a common goal to meet the sea, cohesion for
ever,

And now, the river, a determined force,
With one aim in mind pushes forwards, its

course,
ever downwards, steady, deceptive.
For its surface looks smooth, calm, not festive,
No one sees the turbulence, currents, pushing,
urging, "Move on to the sea,
For our aim is waves to be,"

Nothing stands in the way of such power,
So many raindrops joined together,
And here, at last, is the estuary, churning,
Leaping and greeting,
The tiny drops become as one,
A mighty ocean, free to roam,
With no rulers but the moon and the sun,
To guide them on.

The World Is My Church

My church is the world,
For when I stand beneath the trees,
Or from a cliff, watch tumultuous seas,
When, in the fields, I hear the bees,
Or pick up scents on a wandering breeze,

I give thanks.

My heart fills with joy,
As I raise my eyes to clear blue skies,
Or feel a glow from a golden sunrise,
Laugh with delight at dancing butterflies,
And feel amazed by armoured woodlice,

And I feel alive.

I feel awe,

At how the world fits together,
How the soil of the land, and air and water,
Using days, longer and shorter,
To give seasons, food and shelter,
All in the balance of nature,

And I give thanks,

But still I love to visit churches,
And sit, bathed in the quietness of many
centuries,
Overlaid like layers of dust,

Emotion absorbed by stone strong walls,
And echoed back from silent stalls,
While the glinted glass, witness to all,
Reflects the laughter, joy and tears,

Of hundreds and hundreds and hundreds of
years,
If God made the world, and he still
watches,
Surely he wants us out there, in practice,
Taking care of our planet, the things he
gave us,

Not just sitting in church and giving praises,
So, when we finish our Sunday service,
Please, walk, don't drive,
Let nature thrive,
Put on a sweater instead of the boiler,
So all earth's living, wondrous things
survive.

Robin

As I was digging up the weeds,
And trying to stop the bittercress seeds,
I perceived a robin in a tree,
Its beady eye was watching me,

I sang a song quite quietly,
Of wishing things in harmony,
The robin listened for a while,
Then joined in, professional style,
A song of perfect togetherness,
Entwining tunes, melodious,

It urged me, dig a little more,
To release its food from earth's great store,
Then flew down to my feet,
Selecting grubs, the best to eat,
Removing pests from round my plants,
So they can grow with elegance,

A microcosm of our world,
A benefit to me and bird,
So, all the world, Let's sing in harmony,
For a forever earth, for animals, plants, for
you and me,

Grief

Grief shoots like an arrow to the heart,
Colours fade and all seems dark,
All in the world is once removed,
A blankness in the mind that dulls the mood,

"Be patient", they say,
Time heals all, just keep plodding through
each day,
And as the earth turns and turns,
A speck at the end of the tunnel burns,
A candle glow will melt the grief,
Seven hundred turns and happiness buds like
a new green leaf,

The scales will fall and life green spreads,
The warmth of the sun clears our heads,
Scents come stronger to release the chains,
And the ice round our hearts thaws and
drains,

We'll never forget those people we've loved,
They're part of us now through smooth and
rough,
In the way we think, the things we do,
They'll be memories and thought of all we've
been through.
But as grief dissolves, remember with smiles,
You'll one day laugh again, just wait a while,

Storm Sailing

Wind whistling, water foaming, spray hissing,
We fly,
Mountains looming, trees bending, waves
mounting.
Blue sky,

Go swift, skim on air,
Let's fly together, we do not care,
What lies before us? Is there danger there?
Speed on my beauty, but beware,beware,

A clap of thundering sails behind us,
A hiss of boat riding wave,
What gust of wind is this they are flying?
And then the SMACK! Of sail on water
The wind comes. Be brave

Can my boat and I go faster?
White blazing sail, stretched and taut,
Can't sit sternwards any further,
Gust hits, hull lifts, balance flat our only
thought,

And we and the wind are one

Lucky

I'm lucky to have this world all around me,
Full of birds and animals, fields and trees,
I'm lucky to have the time to see,
Twittering birds at my feeders and loads of
flowers, even bees,

Butterflies flutter in glamorous colours,
A kingfisher flashes in speed numbing blue,
And singing, unseen a myriad voices,
Whistle the songs that say Spring's here
anew,

Oh please, dashing people, just stop for a
moment,
And take a look at this beautiful world,
Gaze at the sunrise, or, if you like, sunset,
A wonderful gift for you to behold,

And then, take that moment and share it
with others,
Show them the beauty that filled you with
awe,
And let the birds singing fill you with
gladness,
It's amazing what nature has hidden in
store,

46

The Moon

As I draw the curtains on a moonlit night,
It sets my memories alight,
Of emotion filled nights gone by,
Under that pure, cold light so high,

The night I lost my job was one,
Pounding the streets, asking what went
wrong?
Empty and tired, I dropped by the stream,
And asked myself why? What does it all
mean?

The moon gave out its serious glow,
Nature calmed me with the water's flow,
And after a while I went home and slept,
Serene after all the tears I had wept,

Happy memories follow of a scent filled
night,
On a holiday when all went right,
We sailed in boats and walked the hills,
And slept in a tent in a moonglinting field,

Some nights were happy, some nights were
sad,
Some gave me calmness when things went
bad,
The moon and the stars, detached above,
Throwing light on tears and laughter and
love.

The Cat

When he was three, he adopted me,
came through my window and jumped on me,
And though I put him firmly out,
He came right back, showing he'd no doubt,
Of where he wanted to live from now,
This house, this person, and, yes, right now,

It took him a year to convince me,

That he had no other home, no family,
That cared and would miss him very badly,
Before I said, "OK. Live with me"

And now we are inseparable,
He greets me home every day,
Looks after the house in his cattish way,
Sits on my chest and purrs to say,
We are the best of friends, undoubtedly,

And what we value most together,
Are the important things as he taught me,
Love for each other, respect and care,
Food, water, comfort and warm shelter

And I realised how lucky we are,
For we have all that and more,
Light, heat, family, friends and security,
People to keep me safe, people to look
after me,
And best of all, that wise young cat to live
with me,

When I see human with human,
There's no peace, no harmony,
Even people who have loved,
Cry out, in anger, grief or jealousy,

And greed claims all and destroys where
love could be,

But when I see humans with their pets,
I see pride and love,
Care and compassion,
Animal and human giving love devotedly,

Is it because animals give their love, no
strings attached?
And show their gratitude unstintingly?
With loyalty strong, they give us strength,
What else can we learn from our wonderful
pets?

Bonds of Love

I've learned a lot these past three weeks,
Of bonds of love, and trust and care,
My cat was hit by a car, you see,
And I have so missed having him home with
me,

No neighbours home, I own no car,
The dash to the vets an unreality,
He seemed so light, so quiet too,
"Hang in there, I'll get you through,"

No surprise, the news was bad,
Two broken legs, "Go home now," they
said,
We'll ring you soon,
He's in shock but we'll see what we can do,"
I kiss my cat, stroke his head,
Didn't want to leave, "Don't die on me," I
said,

They ring me later, I cry and cry
He's on a drip, he might not die,
A lonely sleepless night, the first of many,
I realise he's an integral part of me,

Seeking solace in fields of beauty,
The dazzling light seems grey and gloomy,
And the house I return to feels so empty,
"Please come home to me,"
I shout and shout so desperately,

He's home,
My lovely, trusting three legged cat,
Brought back to me,
I close my eyes in gratitude and from deep within,
A smile begins, I raise my arms with glee,
And now I shout "Whoopee"

54

Beginning of the End

They're going to take our hills away,
And bury them in bricks,
They're going to take the trees away,
Every branch and stick,

They're going to take the grass away,
And every single bloom,
They'll cover it in houses
And spread a mass of gloom,

When we start to suffocate,
And anger rules the world,
They'll see the error of their ways,
When earth's anger is unfurled,

Floods will drown and rivers roar,
Winds will howl and sun will scorch,
Earthquakes shake, and thunder rumble,
And the human world? It crumbles.

War Torn

Under the table I'm safe, I say,
They will not harm me here,
For there's nowhere else for me to go,
Nowhere to run away from fear,

Under the table I'm safe, I whisper,
But in the darkness I hear,
The rumble of tanks approaching,
I think they are getting near,

Under the table I'm safe, I whimper,
As my mother sheds a tear,
For the tanks have ceased their rumble,
When will the soldiers appear?

Under the table I'm safe, I cry
As a shell hits the ground with a roar,
The earth moves, it vibrates,
The table, it shakes,
I can't breath in the dust filled air,

Under the table I'm safe, I sob,
We're farmers and I'm only four,
And my world is now shattered,
The table is gone and my mother lies dead on
the floor,

Nature's Way

Lying in the branches of the tall beech tree,
Stillness keeps me secret, no one sees me,
But I can watch the world roll by,
While I imagine I can fly,

I'll soar like an eagle,
Or hover kestrel like,
Dive like a peregrine,
Near the speed of light,

A blackbird perches in the green glimmer rays,
Unaware of me in the dappled shade,
But I watch in awe, amazed
Every beautiful feather in the sun rays' blaze.

In this natural world of peace,
There's no mad anger, no craziness,
Just the muted roar of wind through
leaves,
And elation filling me.

The Gardener's Tale

You'd think to be a gardener,
The most important skill
Is a horticultural knowledge
But, I soon learnt there's still
Many other skills I need
Besides a knowledge of the weeds
And flowers, shrubs and trees

One needs to know how the world fits
together
The birds and bees, pollination, the weather
The structure of soil, use of irrigation
And the damage man does with insecticides,

herbicides, soil contamination
Not to mention the spread of infection.

One also needs to understand the people

Every person different, they say
And I have seen this true in many ways
Let's take a look at those horrible weeds
Like dandelions with their proliferous seeds,
Except, their flower is bright, leaf is salad, the
roots make coffee ,
So, in a self sufficient garden its allowed to
grow, free

Nettles are welcome in some of the places
For the butterfly's eggs, their caterpillars
voracious
They hatch and need this natural food
And fly as butterflies to lift our mood

Nine weeds I can name
that are flowers in gardens of mine

Forget-me-not, violet, buttercup, celandine
Bindweed (I shudder), sorrel, teasel, feverfew
and columbine

The preciseness of detail varies greatly
With one garden perfect balls, pots in
symmetry,
No leaves with holes, no brown edges to see
A pigeon evicted from the apple tree
For discarding materials brought by its mate
Twigs below standard for her perfectionist
trait,

Another lady's front garden is all cubes and squares
Lonicera, choisya, lavender blocks, even spireas
But the back garden's a profusion of carefree flowers
With a bed of buttercups, ox eye daisies, rambling rose bowers
Climbers scrambling around shrubs with stature,

This garden twins a plot designed for nature,
Where wildflowers are sown for buzzing bees
And the ground is strewn with many old
leaves
Left for creatures like slugs and snails
There are ladybirds sleeping and hedgehog
trails
Seedheads are left for goldfinches to eat
Nothing is tidy, nothing is neat
Discussions were held over tumbling
climbers
Taking the light from shrubs that aren't
rhymers
"For nests," she said,
But I said:
"Their beds can be smaller and your shrubs a
bit smarter,"
And now the garden is still for nature
And the plants enjoyed by their creator

Going on with the subject of what's weeds,
what's flowers
the jury's out on aquilegias,
One lady, she points with disgust, "That's a
weed,"
While another man greedily collects all the
seed
"Grannies bonnet's so beautiful" he says with
a smile
Good value for money for it flowers a long
while

"Are violets a weed here?" I asked one chap
He raised his hand and scratched his cap
"Nothing's a weed here until I've seen its
flower",
He said with a smile that was kind of dour,
And so we grew buttercups, the colour of
gold
And left alone dandelions yellow and bold
The violets spread over all of the ground
And scarlet pimpernel made a bright red
mound,
And in buzzed the bees, to enjoy a great
feast
While birds fed on teasel, Oh what a treat

I have a customer, his name is Dave,
And over fuchsias he does rave,
Six foot tall, he rarely bends,
So hanging baskets are what tends,
to matter most
Adorning posts
But the lawn is rarely mown
Because you see, he never looks down.
When I did eventually mow,
His neighbour cried "Well what do you know?
Dave's garden's tidy yo-ho-ho

Psychology's a useful skill
For bending someone's mind who still
With enthusiasm sprays to kill
The pests that, if left, ladybirds will,
And lacewings too,
Balancing nature as they take their fill,

This skill is useful, too, for marriage guidance, pets
And grandparents who have youngsters gone off the tracks,

"Pets?" You say, "What do you mean?"
Distracting the cat that plays with shears
And the dog who nicks my secateurs
And then there's the clever hen
Who knows how to escape her pen
Her companion is not so bright
And thinks my shoelaces when in sight
Are worms to peck, they don't taste nice
But still she tries
Its so unwise,

Other dogs are so friendly, saying "Shall I lick your face
While you're sharing my lovely space?
Can you throw my ball for me to chase?
And here's the ball for you to throw
Again, and now you can have another go"

But what about the marriage thing?
On this I have 2 tales to spin.
To plan the garden, I ask what colours they like their flowers
"Oh, we like pink and purple and blue,"
The guy says,"Don't we darling Sue."
"Oh, I like yellow and orange and red,
Dear Fred,
They make a lovely, cheerful bed,"
To stop the argument gaining pace,
I design one side in blues, one side in reds
With chairs to face
Their favourite space
Preventing marital disgrace

In my other case,
The problem lies
In whether gardens should be formal,
defined,
Lines of shrubs upright,
Not a wildflower in sight
A Chinese garden if you will,
Everything symmetrical
But the husband's different, an Englishman
Who throws wild seed with wild abandon

He likes his flowers anywhere
And colours mixed, he does not care,

To keep the peace
My solution is:
Symmetrical beds
Incorporating flowers in reds
And pinks and yellows and blue,
And maybe even orange too
But every flower is carefully placed
So that nature's symmetry's embraced.

What of the child gone off the tracks?
Sometimes attention's what he lacks
Sometimes, too much energy still
After sitting still all day in school
So let's have a child's garden now
Where they can dig and sow and plough
And plant their seeds and see them grow
With grandma's praise and a smile bestowed
Energy spent out in the sun,

And a new relationship's begun,

One day as I cycled from shade to sun and
sun to shade
The skill I needed was my first aid
For up ahead, a van, with drivers door
undone
blocked the road and on the floor, a man
lay still.
I thought, what's happened here?
And practically pushed down my fear
A woman stood above the man
as if a statue cold, frozen
I looked more carefully at the lad
and saw with shock, he had no head
No head,?
My brain revved up a gear
Cycled harder, I was nearly there
Nothing I could do for the man with no head
But the lady's in shock , I'd help her instead

Pull her away from the terrible sight
Get her sweet tea to reduce her fright

Call nine, nine nine for an ambulance crew
Not much else I really could do
Then, as I reached the van I saw
It said on the side, Severn,& Trent Water

And the man raised his head from a hole in
the ground
I felt weak at the knees and my heart gave a
bound
No emergency here, I thought feeling gay
I'll save my first aid for another day
All he was doing was reading the meter.

Those climbing skills I'd thought I'd need
Are not just for the apple trees
But for climbing gates and fences too
For customers who are in a stew

I hear a voice through the letterbox
"I've lost my keys, can't undo the locks,"
"No problem," say I, "I'll climb the gate,

By the back door you can wait,"
So round the back I run at speed
Climb the gate, then start to weed
I hope that in an hour or so
Key found, out through the house I'll go.

Another house, the owner cried
"My cat is lost, I've looked far and wide,"
But when outside, I could hear "MEEOW,
I need help and I need it now"
I called the owner, "I can hear her cry,
Over there somewhere, I wonder why."
The owner ran off down the road,
"I know which house but no one's home,
They don't come home 'til six at night,
Oh Annie, Annie, What a plight"

ANNIE'S THE CAT

The lady had a ladder, we made a plan
If no one's home, break in I can,
rescue your cat and then be gone

We carried the ladder down the street,
"You're sure no one's home until too late?"
"Yes," the owner said, "I'm sure,
but just in case I'll knock the door"
No one came, I scaled the ladder,
But as I put my foot upon the gate and
looked to see
If I could exit easily
A voice said, "Er Excuse me,"
The owner is standing with a frown
And from the ladder I get down
"The lady's cat's stuck in your garden
His frown's replaced with sudden laughter
Then round the garden we chase the puss
Until she's captured in a viburnum bush

One time on climbing o'er the gate
I called myself an ID DEE OT
You see, the toggle of my coat
Slid down a gap between two slats
And firmly held me, couldn't move
To get that toggle from the groove
Nothing to climb on to rescale the gate
How to get out of that terrible plight?
Couldn't reach a tool to cut me free
In the end, took my coat off – solution EASY

My transport's a bike
Which I really like
But sometimes I get a really bad fright
One day I was cycling along a main road
Van coming from my left with quite a big
load
I saw him look, it seemed my way
But as I passed, his engine revved, he drove
towards me, no delay
I swerved out to the centre line

Dodged the bonnet with its model sign
Phew I thought,.I'm in the clear,
But his wing mirror hooked my ear
And as the van, it changed its gear
I accelerated, couldn't get clear
I didn't dare knock on his door for fear
Of my handlebars turning, Oh dear, Oh dear,
The driver must have got a fright
On looking right
A cyclist hooked, oh what a sight

He put his foot upon the brake
But I couldn't stop. I couldn't wait,
My bike sailed on for half a mile
He leapt from his van, then after a while
called "Are you alright?" I raised a smile
"Still alive and pedalling, you won't stand
trial."

Dementia in some, or moving house often
Can lead, I find to considerable confusion
Given the wrong house number, I weed 35
with no answer to the bell, I think, she'll
arrive,
After no one comes home, I put a note
through the door
Job done, please ring me, if your bus made
you late, I'm sorry, I'm sure
"Hello," said a voice when I answered my
phone
"Nice job in the garden, but I hope you won't
moan
It's my neighbour who wants you, she's done
this before
Mixing up numbers. She's in fact 34"

Poor memory's a condition that makes
people sad
But for one of my clients it made me feel
glad
I wonder if you remember being six years old
when each new thing you learned was like
silver and gold,
Amazing, exciting, a magical world,

For four years with this lady, the daffodils
grew
then flowered and died and she wanted
something new
"Throw those away", she said
"Now they are dead",
but I said,
"If we plant them in the garden,
They'll flower again each year"
The lady's smile grew bigger
As she said with happy cheer
"Well, I never knew that,
Well fancy that

what a really wonderful thing"
And I saw there was advantage
If you're good at forgetting.

At another house, no boundary between her
and next door
I weed along happily my employment for an
hour
When my client appears, she cries out "What
a laugh,
You've done mine and the neighbours in the
time I'd have done half"

On technology, I'm a failure
'Though I often do get asked
"Do you know why my mobiles not working
Can you help with a computer task?"
Well, sometimes the answer is easy
If the plug is not switched on
Or its solved by switching it all off
and then just switching on

Sometimes there's a book with answers
A diagram to read
But if its experience I'm needing
I'm afraid I won't succeed

I'd like to mention map reading's a useful
skill to have
'cos on my bike there's no battery to run a
new satnav
And sometimes customers don't know their
left hand from their right
Or forget the house gate on the corner
changed colour from blue to white
So as directions can get you lost
Its a good idea to know
Which way is south, north, east or west
so on the map, I know which route is best

I'm sometimes asked about nature What's
that bird up in the tree?
Could a deer jump o'er my fence and eat up
all my peas
Do the foxes hibernate?

And what for a hedgehog is a safe winter
weight?
Do you think that hole by the lake,
is the home of a mole or a rattle snake?
I don't know all the answers
But I quite like finding out
It's good to know there's a book to read
whenever I'm in doubt

DIY skills, I have needed
When the garden's dug and weeded
Can you fix my toilet? Its flooding
everywhere.
And can you paint my fence now? Its looking
kind of bare
Are you good at woodwork, the pagodas
fallen down?

I have a pipe that's struck a leak, its flooding all the lawn.

Can you make my bench seat that my son sent from IKEA?

Can you dig my pond out and I'd like a little weir.

Luckily my dad, he was an engineer

And at five years old he'd taught me how to use a saw

By eight years old, he'd shown us how to paint and how to drill

So I can make a temporary fix 'til the professionals bring their skill

Diplomacy's a skill I found
Hard to learn, I'm world renowned
For bluntly saying what's in my head
Not thinking how it should be said
Luckily, I've learned new ways
So when I'm told to prune the roses
In September and I'm thinking "Golly Moses,
There's still a month of flowers to bloom
With climate change, it's much too soon
I now explain why the books aren't right
Say, we're lucky now to enjoy the sight
Of roses flowering for 30 more days
With October now resembling September's
ways

I've found that by explaining things
And listening to what my customer thinks,
I can leave behind many smiling faces
As they look at their healthy joyful spaces

I think, you know, the world would be

A happier place for you and me
If everyone could learn the art
Of politeness and diplomacy,

Languages are a needed skill
For gardening in wild Portugal
Where a client has a villa
The locals always said "Manana"
When she asked "When will you dig?
Plant my lemon tree and my fig"
So she asked me "Will you stay,
In the villa for a week of course we'll pay?"
In a villa with a pool?
To turn this down I'd be a fool
They paid my fare, provided food
I had a lovely time, worked hard
Seeing the garden taking form
On a hillside, the air was warm
The scent of olives in the air
Changing the land to blooms from bare
And spoke my Portuguese in shops

To buy a rake. My work didn't stop
Until the villa stood surrounded
with flowers galore, the neighbours
astounded

In gardening there's a cycle of growth
Every year new seeds grow to flowers, then
die, become earth
The earth feeds the roots as new flowers
grow, throw their seeds and in cycle, create
new birth
I feel sadness so often as customers die
Those left behind feeling lonely ask "why?"
That cycle of grief, feeling angry then blank,
either frenetic energy or tired and sad
It helps to know that energy never ever dies
The energy of character will revive and then
thrive
In the generations that follow, they'll always
be alive

I work in gardens as small as just one bed
Each centimetre's valued, filled with blue and
white and red
I work in other gardens as big as stately
homes
I'm awed by the splendour, by the space that
I can roam
But all gardens are special, I know this for
sure,
So come out in the sunshine, come open
your door

Nature is beautiful, It makes your heart sing
Every flower in the garden, every bird on the wing
The last thought I'll leave as I put down my pen

Please, Look after our world for our children's children.

Cat Meeting

I went out walking one moonlit night,
To look at the stars, oh what a sight,
Despite the month, the night was warm,
And I walked slowly, enjoying the balm
I climbed onto a grassy hill,
Gazing up at the sky so filled
With pinpricks of light,
Their sparkles slight
But Oh so many, many worlds
Winking at me. I'm without words,
Just sigh at so much beauty there
Reducing my worries and my cares,

Then I feel I'm being watched
And look around to see what's what
Around my feet, seven cats just sit
They exchange the thought, Who is this twit?
Standing on our special hill
Reserved for when we need to meet
And talk the serious things of cats

Beneath the stars, of this and that,

Their almond eyes all study me
And the lead cat moves its head decisively,
"We're having a meeting, can't you see?
Its private for cats, we're talking secretly",

I duck my head in apology
And give my regrets, "I'm so sorry.
I'll go now, shall I?" I ask the cat,
Approval given I step carefully back
And descend the hill with cat approval
Removing myself from cat perusal
I feel their thoughts dismissing me
And the meeting continues instantly

I smile quietly and heading home,
to bed,
Think I would like to be a cat on the hill
beneath the moon and stars instead.

Bad Day

You know those days when things go wrong
When you wish the day was not so long,
When bag handles fail so that apples roll
To the bottom of the hill ending black as coal
And the bus pulls out and drives away
Passengers give an ironic wave
Unexpected rain showers fall
When you have no coat at all
and when you look down at your shoes
You realise ones red, one blue
And then you lose your front door key
Slipped from your pocket possibly
You search the road carefully
And down the drain there's something silvery,
Of all the places to drop the thing
I poke in sticks try to catch the ring
It hooks, I lift, try not to breathe
Get it clear from a lump of leaves
But now I can't get a finger in

The gap between is far too thin
And, then when in despair I cry
Enough's enough, nothing more I'll try
Don't test me more, I've failed, I know
Shake a fist at the sky, I feel so low,
And round the corner a saviour comes,
A six year old child with tiny thumbs
She easily reaches to get my key
And now I'm home can get my tea
And a jam tart, too for that little girl
A jewel in the crown, a tiny pearl,
The day is over . I've made it through
And tomorrow will dawn, a clean sheet, all
new,

Qualities

There are many qualities of the human race,
But which are those that I embrace?
Which value most in those I meet?
Qualities I'd like to emulate,

Honesty, joy, consideration,
Wisdom shared, in moderation,
Demonstration of care and kindness,
The ability to spread happiness,

Courage in adversity,
Appreciating nature's beauty,
Spreading peace and tranquillity,
Pure goodness. What a quality,

Theses are the things I hope endure,
To keep the future world secure,

Charlie Cushion

Charlie cushion is my greatest friend.
He's very soft from end to end,
He has a special tail and face,
And in between there's lots of space,

For a cat like me. To curl up tight,
And purr and purr with all my might,
We sit in the sun, so warm together,
I'll love him every day forever,

Charlie cushion was made for me,
By a very special, smart lady,
Who did a lot of work, clearly,
To keep me happy as can be,
"Thank you," I smile gratefully,

Magic Remembered

We creep downstairs so silently,
(I think that I am maybe three),
Christmas excitement is surrounding me,
Enfolding me in gusts of glee,

"Dad's asleep", Mother warns,
"So we must do everything quietly,"
We nod our heads most seriously,
And then the door is opened so we can see
the tree,
We jump with joy, try not to shout, for the
tree is lit up magically,

And underneath the tree, presents stacked
haphazardly,
But one present, so big, it isn't wrapped, you
see,
And I can see a go-cart, especially for me,
It's only wrapped in tinsel which glitters
brilliantly,

THANK YOU Father Christmas,
THANK YOU Mum and Dad,
For I know they all helped in bringing me,
That very special present,
That present just for me,

Cats

Cats are special,
Cats are wise,
Cats are furry,
With big bright eyes,

Cats are elegant,
Such beauty, such grace,
Strong in character,
Endearing face,

A house with a cat,
Is an honoured place,
It emanates welcome,
With contented happiness,

A house with a cat,
is affection filled,
In achieving this.

A cat is most highly skilled,

How did the amazing cat attain,
Its perfect balance, its exceptional brain,
Those super paws, that rumbling purr,
All wrapped in a loving bundle of fur?

A Giving Time

It's year end, it's Christmas time,
And as I walk passed the church and see its
sign,
I think of the mix of legend, myth and rhyme.
That, behind our present day pleasures, lie,

And wonder how it came to this.

First, a pagan festival of thanksgiving,
Midwinter gone, light returning,
St Nicholas giving presents to the town's
children,
And Jesus in the manger, who knew what he
would do then,
And , you know what matters
is we live in love,
Give peace and care and thanks for what we
have,

But, is that now what happens at our English
Christmas time?
What I see so often is greed, jealousy and
gluttony,
No joy in giving, due to fear of debt,
No sharing of burdens, just take, take, take.

Well.

Can I ask, this Christmas, that you take a
moments break,
to teach the children as they wake,
the joy of giving,
Not just receiving,
For yourselves, your family and the future's
sake,

Margot Bish has now written eight books and is working on the ninth as this goes to print. She lives in Redditch with a cat who loves to show her expertise in both writing and computers and has contributed greatly to this compilation.

Other books include:

<u>For Children</u>
How Could I Forget?
The Perfect Home
The Long Day Out
Through The Storm

<u>For Teenagers and Adults</u>
A Difficult Age (short story)

Tis The Irish Way (short story)

A Moment In Time (novel)

.

Printed in Great Britain
by Amazon

11212467R00068